This book belongs to:

.................................................

.................................................

*For my mother, who filled our home with books*

*— L.M.*

*I want to dedicate this book to my parents,*
*who always encouraged me to be*
*the very best version of myself. And to my sister,*
*Audrey, for years and years of free therapy.*

*—C.B.*

Text copyright © 2020 by Lori Mortensen

Illustrations copyright © 2020 by Chloe Bristol

Edward Gorey photo in Author's Note © 1977 by Jack Mitchell/Getty Images

Versify is an imprint of Houghton Mifflin Harcourt Publishing Company.

hmhbooks.com

The illustrations in this book were done in pencil and painted digitally.

The text type was set in IM Fell DW Pica.

Library of Congress Cataloging-in-Publication Data

Names: Mortensen, Lori, 1955– author. | Bristol, Chloe, illustrator.

Title: Nonsense! : the curious story of Edward Gorey / Lori Mortensen ; illustrated by Chloe Bristol.

Description: Boston : Houghton Mifflin Harcourt, 2020. | Audience: Ages 4–7 |

Audience: K to Grade 3 | Identifiers: LCCN 2019008793 | ISBN 9780358033684 (hardcover picture book)

Subjects: LCSH: Gorey, Edward, 1925–2000—Juvenile literature. | Illustrators—United States—Biography—

Juvenile literature. | Authors, American—20th century—Biography—Juvenile literature.

Classification: LCC NX512.G67 M67 2020 | DDC 741.6092 [B]—dc23

LC record available at https://lccn.loc.gov/2019008793

Manufactured in China

SCP 10 9 8 7 6 5 4 3 2 1

4500786545

# NONSENSE!

## The Curious Story of EDWARD GOREY

Written by
Lori Mortensen

Illustrated by
Chloe Bristol

VERSIFY
Houghton Mifflin Harcourt
Boston   New York

# Greetings, Dear Reader!

Since you are reading this book,
it's as clear as the dimple on your chin
that you love words and pictures.

And pictures and words!
(Such nonsense!)

In 1925, a boy was born
in Chicago
who loved words
and pictures, too.
A brilliant boy.
An only boy.
A dandy boy who looked out
his window,
drew sausage-shaped pictures
of city-bound trains,
and taught himself to read.

And oh, did he read!
He gobbled up adventures
and mysteries.
Comics and poetry.
The entire works
of French novelist
Victor Hugo,
for goodness' sake.
(Remember *The Hunchback
of Notre Dame*?
That's *him!*)

Then, one day, young Edward read
the whimsical *Alice in Wonderland*
and the frightfully gruesome *Dracula,*
one after the other.

A strange combination
that captured his imagination like
a penguin sipping tea
on a runaway train.

For you see,
while *Alice* was quaint and curious,
*Dracula* was dark and disturbing.
This would change his life.

Oh, pardon me.

Did I mention?

His name was Edward Gorey.

Did it change his life all at once?
No, it did not. As you may have noticed,
many things do not happen all at once.

First, bright young Edward
skipped grades—SKIP, SKIP, SKIP—
and moved with his family a dozen times—
1, 2, 3, 4, 5, 6, 7, 8, 9, 10, 11, 12.
(Heavens to Betsy! That's a lot!)

Young Edward scribbled and sketched,
sketched and scribbled, wherever he went.

Then, before he knew it,

eighteen-year-old Edward was drafted into the army.

An army full of rules,

where Company Clerk Edward

filed dreary reports, one after another.

"It was a ghastly place," he later recalled.

By the time
tall,
skinny,
furry-coated,
ring-fingered,
sneaker-footed Edward
arrived at Harvard,
he was following his own rules,
so different
from the campus crowds
that passed him by
in stuffy white shirts and ties.

Who was that "tall and spooky" chap?

But it was just Edward
being Edward,
with a hatful of nonsense thrown in.

So did those sweet and sinister books he'd read
change his life *now?*
No, they did not.
But isn't patience a lovely thing?

You see, at Harvard
Edward mingled
with other writers and poets
just like him,
who tried on the arts
like a trunkful of clothes.
Poems.
Plays.
Prose.
Edward wrote them all.

Did he know what he wanted
to do with his life?

Alas and alack,
he did not.

In 1953,
Edward moved to New York,
and got a job in the art department
of a big book publisher.

During the day,
Edward worked on everyone else's books,
laying out pages,
drawing letters by hand,
designing book covers,
and illustrating.

Then one day . . .

. . . Edward stopped
and thought.

**What about the books**
*he* **wanted to write?**

That's when it happened.

# Voilà!

After work,
Edward scribbled down stories
the way he wanted to write them.

When he finished a story,
he illustrated each scene
with a slow and careful hand.

Stories that mingled
sweetness and innocence,
danger and darkness,
all mixed up
with his own brand of silliness.

When publishers turned him down,
Edward launched his own company, Fantod Press.

No one had ever seen books
like Edward's before.

He wrote strange stories
with curious titles like

*The Unstrung Harp,*

*The Abandoned Sock,*

*The Wuggly Ump,*

*The Galoshes of Remorse,*

and *The Gashlycrumb Tinies,*

the worst sort of alphabet tale that began:

*A is for Amy who fell down the stairs*

*B is for Basil assaulted by bears*

*C is for Clara who wasted away*

*D is for Desmond thrown out of a sleigh*

Instead of drawing
colorful, happy-go-lucky pictures,
Edward used pen and ink
to draw seas of sketchy black lines,
as if the stories were set
in a time and place long ago.

Instead of publishing books with his real name,

# Edward Gorey,

he often mixed the letters up in anagrams,
making silly new names like

Odgred Weary

Dreary Wodge

Regera Dowdy

E. G. Deadworry

Garrod Weedy

Drew Dogyear

Edgar E. Wordy

Roy Grewdead

Wardore Edgy

Wee Graddory

Ydora Wredge

(My goodness! How many names could there be?)
Names as silly as the ones in his books:

Octavia Prong,

Williboo Lake,

Waffle, Skrump,

Humglum, and Crunk.

It was all part of the nonsense.

Some people did not like his stories.
Why would anyone write stories
with such odd and unfortunate endings?

His book *The Beastly Baby*
made some mothers so mad
they ripped it to shreds and
mailed it back to him.
HARRUMPH!

But Edward liked writing and illustrating
stories that made readers uneasy.

To Edward,
the world was an uncertain place
where anything might happen.
And in Edward's stories, it did!

Anything less would be boring.
And who wanted that?
Not Edward.

People often asked him what his stories meant.

But Edward didn't like explaining this and that.

He thought readers should use
their own imaginations.

It would be "the height of folly"
to take his work seriously, he said.

So tall,
skinny,
furry-coated,
ring-fingered,
sneaker-footed
Edward wrote stories
with sketchy black lines,
just the way he imagined them.

It was just Edward

being Edward,

with a hatful of nonsense thrown in.

# Author's Note

Edward St. John Gorey was born on February 22, 1925, in Chicago, Illinois. A child prodigy, he began drawing by the age of one and a half and taught himself to read by the age of three. Since his books have a dark side, people think he must have had a tragic childhood too. But Gorey admitted his was as happy as anyone's and included playing neighborhood games of kick the can and Monopoly, going to the movies, and reading all kinds of books from comics to horror. His favorites included *The Secret Garden* by Frances Hodgson Burnett, books by A. A. Milne, and Agatha Christie mysteries.

In ninth grade, Gorey attended Chicago's legendary Francis Parker School, where his talents began to shine. His work appeared in school exhibits and publications, and one of his cartoons was published in the sports section of a Chicago newspaper when he was thirteen years old.

After graduation, Gorey was offered a scholarship to Harvard, but World War II put his plans on hold. In 1943, Gorey served as a company clerk at Dugway Proving Ground in Utah for two years.

In 1946, Gorey enrolled at Harvard. It was here that he began mingling with a community of artists, writers, and poets and took creative writing classes.

After graduating in 1950—"I didn't envision a career in anything," said Gorey—he eventually took a part-time job at a Boston bookstore and tried his hand at writing novels that he never finished. Two years later, Gorey moved to New York and got a job in the art department at Doubleday. It was an important step. After working month after month on other people's projects, Gorey decided to write and illustrate his own books. His first book, *The Unstrung Harp,* was published in 1953. It was an illustrated tale about a brooding Mr. Earbrass who struggled to write a novel just like he did.

Gorey published over one hundred books and illustrated over sixty books by other authors, including Charles Dickens, Lewis Carroll, T. S. Eliot, and John Ciardi, his former teacher. Although Gorey's work appeals to all ages, only a few of his books, such as *The Wuggly Ump* and *The Bug Book,* were specifically written for children.

Gorey's passion for ballet was almost as strong as his passion for writing and illustrating. While he was in New York, he attended every performance of the New York City Ballet for twenty-three seasons. Many of his illustrated characters share the same long, graceful lines as the dancers he watched.

Throughout his adult life, Gorey's appearance was as striking as his work. Over six feet tall, his long fur coats, Converse sneakers, heavy jewelry, and metal rings made him easily recognizable wherever he went. Friends, colleagues, and critics offered many colorful descriptions from "buccaneer" to "bongo-drumming beatnik" to "full-blown eccentric" to "an immigrant from another century." Later in life, Gorey gave up his fur coats and became an avid supporter of animal rights.

Although Gorey enjoyed friendships, he preferred solitude and lived his life precisely as he pleased. In 1979, Gorey bought a two-hundred-year-old sea captain's home in Cape Cod, also called the Elephant House, that he shared with a beloved covey of cats and an astounding number of collections of things, such as doorknobs, potato mashers, cheese graters, tiny teddy bears, rocks, frogs, and a library of twenty-five thousand books. In 2000, seventy-five-year-old Edward Gorey passed away. His house was turned into a museum. When asked about his work, he often gave vague and mysterious answers. "Is there anything people don't understand about you?" an interviewer once asked. "Yes . . . no," Gorey replied.

Today, Gorey's sweet and sinister style continues to have a profound effect. Lemony Snicket's A Series of Unfortunate Events, Tim Burton's *The Nightmare Before Christmas*, and Neil Gaiman's *Coraline* must all tip their hats to Edward Gorey.

Will the curious story of Edward Gorey ever end?

Nonsense.

# Sources

**Internet:**

Biography.com. "Edward Gorey Biography." April 1, 2014. www.biography.com/people/edward-gorey-40616

Dery, Mark. "Nightshade Is Growing Like Weeds." *New York Times*. March 2, 2011. www.nytimes.com/2011/03/06/arts/design/06gorey.html

The Edward Gorey House. "From the Macabre to the Meowvelous: 13 Facts About Artist Edward Gorey." Biography.com. October 30, 2014. www.biography.com/news/edward-gorey-biography-facts

The Edward Gorey House. www.edwardgoreyhouse.org

Lumenello, Susan. "Edward Gorey." *Harvard Magazine*. March–April 2007. harvardmagazine.com/2007/03/edward-gorey.html

**Books:**

Gorey, Edward. *Amphigorey Again*. Boston: Harcourt Books, 2006.

Gorey, Edward. *Amphigorey: Fifteen Books*. New York: Penguin Group, 1972.

Gorey, Edward. *Ascending Peculiarity: Edward Gorey on Edward Gorey*. Edited by Karen Wilkin. Boston: Harcourt, Inc., 2001.

Gorey, Edward. *The Gashlycrumb Tinies*. Boston: Harcourt, Brace & Company, 1963.

Theroux, Alexander. *The Strange Case of Edward Gorey*. Seattle: Fantagraphics, 2011.